CRAZY CREATURES OF THE ANIMAL KINGDOM

WHAT DO YOU KNOW ABOUT ANIMALS WITH ARMOR?

FRANCINE TOPACIO

PowerKiDS press.

New York

Published in 2021 by The Rosen Publishing Group, Inc.
29 East 21st Street, New York, NY 10010

First Edition

Portions of this work were originally authored by Marie Racanelli and published as *Animals with Armor*. All new material in this edition authored by Francine Topacio.

Editor: Kara Murray
Book Design: Tanya Dellaccio

Photo Credits: Cover Karthik babu Murugesan/500px/Getty Images; p. 5 Peter Chadwick/Gallo Images/Getty Images; p. 6 John McKeen/Moment/Getty Images; p. 7 PhotocechCZ/Shutterstock.com; p. 8 princessdlaf/E+/Getty Images; p. 9 seasoning_17/Shutterstock.com; p. 10 reptiles4all/Shutterstock.com; p. 11 Christian Lehmann/Shutterstock.com; p. 13 Joel Sartore/National Geographic Image Collection/Getty Images; p. 15 Sloot/iStock/Getty Images; p. 17 TacioPhilip/iStock/Getty Images; p. 18 Ozgur Donmaz/DigitalVision/Getty Images; p. 19 Bozhena Melnyk/Shutterstock.com; p. 21 James Hager/robertharding/Getty Images; p. 22 Life On White/Oxford Scientific/Getty Images.

Library of Congress Cataloging-in-Publication Data

Names: Topacio, Francine, author.
Title: What do you know about animals with armor? / Francine Topacio.
Description: New York : PowerKids Press, [2021] | Series: Crazy creatures of the animal kingdom | Includes index.
Identifiers: LCCN 2019059546 | ISBN 9781725319769 (paperback) | ISBN 9781725319783 (library binding) | ISBN 9781725319776 (6 pack)
Subjects: LCSH: Armored animals—Juvenile literature. | Animal defenses—Juvenile literature.
Classification: LCC QL759 .T67 2021 | DDC 591.47—dc23
LC record available at https://lccn.loc.gov/2019059546

Manufactured in the United States of America

CPSIA Compliance Information: Batch #CSPK20. For Further Information contact Rosen Publishing, New York, New York at 1-800-237-9932.

CONTENTS

ANIMAL ARMOR 4
ARMORED ANIMALS 6
TORTOISES AND TURTLES 8
ARMOR WITH SCALES 10
ALL ABOUT ARMOR 12
ARMORED MAMMALS 14
ARMORED INSECTS 16
SNAILS AND THEIR ARMOR 18
UNDERWATER ANIMALS WITH ARMOR 20
THE IMPORTANCE OF ARMOR 22
GLOSSARY 23
INDEX 24
WEBSITES 24

ANIMAL ARMOR

Animals have different coverings on their bodies. Some have fur. Others have feathers. Some kinds of animals have strong, hard coverings. All these coverings help animals live in their **habitats** in different ways. A bear's fur keeps it warm and dry in its home. A blue jay's feathers help it fly and find a mate.

Why might an animal need a hard, strong covering? Have you ever seen a picture of knights heading into battle? Some animals are born with special coverings that are like the armor worn by knights, such as hard scales, shells, and thick skin. All armor is meant to **protect**. Let's learn more about animals with armor.

Hermit crabs find their own armor! The shells they're born with aren't hard enough to protect their bodies so they must find an empty one to use.

ARMORED ANIMALS

Many animals have developed armor on their bodies as a **defense** against **predators**. You can find them all over the world.

Some animals, like snails and turtles, carry hard shells on their backs. Lobsters and crabs have shells too. Crocodiles and alligators are covered in thick, bony plates and scales. Hippos don't have scales or shells, but they have skin so thick that it can be nearly **impenetrable** to a predator's bite. These animals are so well protected that you might say they walk around wearing their own built-in bodyguards!

HOW STRANGE!

Hippos' skin has another superpower! It lets out something called blood sweat. It's thick and red and keeps the animal safe from sunburn as well as infection from cuts.

Hippos may look like they're too big to move fast, but they can run up to 19 miles (30 km) per hour. They'll attack any animal, including a human, that gets too close.

TORTOISES AND TURTLES

When you picture an animal with a shell, the first animal that pops into your mind might be a turtle or a tortoise. Turtles live in or near water. Tortoises live mostly on land. Neither turtles nor tortoises can crawl out of their shells. Their bodies are attached to their hard coverings. Their shells are made of bone that's covered in thick scales, called scutes. The top of the shell is known as the carapace.

Some turtles and tortoises can pull their heads and legs into their shells when they're in danger. Others can just turn their heads to the side and tuck them right under the edge of the shell.

BOX TURTLE

Two African spurred tortoises rest in their burrow. These tortoises can weigh more than 100 pounds (45 kg). They eat grasses, flowers, and cacti.

ARMOR WITH SCALES

Alligators and crocodiles are kept safe by rows of thick, hard scales. Some of these scales have points or ridges on them. Not only do crocodiles and alligators have thick skin, but they also have bony pieces of armor under their skin. It might not surprise you to hear that adult alligators and crocodiles have very few predators!

Lizards and snakes have tough scales too. The spiny-tailed lizard, which lives in Africa, has a special piece of armor on its hide. It has large, pointed scales on its thick tail. It swings its tail like a club at enemies to keep them away.

HOW STRANGE!

One look at the spikes on the spiny-tailed lizard's tail is enough to keep many predators away! To defend itself, sometimes the lizard will take its tail in its mouth, forming an armored circle.

The Australian saltwater crocodile is a fearsome predator! It has no enemies except for humans and other crocodiles. In fact, it was once hunted by people for its hide and meat.

ALL ABOUT ARMOR

1 A hippo's thick skin is its armor. It keeps it safe from biting insects as well as the much bigger bites of crocodiles and lions.

2 Hippo skin gives off blood sweat, which kills illness-causing **bacteria**. It acts as a sunscreen as well, to protect the hippo's skin from the strong sun in its African home.

3 If a scallop, a kind of shellfish, senses danger, it keeps its shell tightly closed so that its soft body can't be hurt.

4 The largest lobster ever found weighed about 44 pounds (20 kg). Scientists think it was about 100 years old!

5 Snails that live in water have thicker shells than land snails. The water helps the snails carry the weight of their shells.

6 A giant clam can have a shell that is about 4 feet (1 m) wide!

7 The three-banded armadillo can completely curl up into a ball to keep itself safe.

8 A pill millipede can curl up into a ball if it's attacked. The segments of its body fit perfectly together. The armored ball is hard to pull open, so enemies leave it alone.

THREE-BANDED ARMADILLO

ARMORED MAMMALS

Armadillos are **mammals** with very hard coverings. Their name means "little armored one." There are about 20 different kinds of armadillos. Some are so small they fit in the palm of your hand. Others can be as big as a large cat. Their armor is made up of bony plates covered with scales.

A pangolin is another armored mammal. It has large, bony plates all over its body. The plates make it look a bit like a really big walking pinecone! It lives in Africa and Asia. To escape danger, it curls up into a ball. The scales on its tail are sharp, and it can use them to defend itself.

This is a six-banded armadillo, also known as a yellow armadillo. It lives in South America. It gets its name from the six to eight movable bands on its body.

HOW STRANGE!

People often think pangolins are reptiles because of their scales. They are the only mammals that are almost completely covered in scales.

ARMORED INSECTS

Humans have skeletons on the insides of our bodies. Your skeleton is made of bone and helps hold up your body. It grows along with you. Insects, spiders, and some other animals have **exoskeletons**, which support their bodies from the outside. They don't have skeletons inside their bodies. Insects' exoskeletons are generally flexible but strong. The exoskeleton works like armor to keep the animals safe.

Some insects have sharp, tough spikes sticking out of their legs. These give them extra protection. They may also have hairs or scales, as on a butterfly's wings, that help keep them safe.

HOW STRANGE!

Butterflies' wings help keep them from being trapped by spiderwebs! If a butterfly flies into a web, it will lose scales where it is stuck to the web. Then its wings can come unstuck!

Since insects' exoskeletons can't grow, insects, such as this cicada, need to shed them to allow for new, larger ones. This is called **molting**.

SNAILS AND THEIR ARMOR

Snails also are armored animals. Their hard shells protect their soft bodies. Snails are **gastropods**, which are part of the soft-bodied mollusk, or shellfish, family. Only some snails live in the ocean, though. Many kinds of snails may even live in your garden.

Did you know that when a snail breaks out of its egg, it eats the eggshell? A baby snail is born with a very soft shell. For the shell to grow harder, the snail must eat lots of **calcium**, which the eggshell has plenty of. The shell grows as the snail grows larger. The shell grows into a spiral shape. Snails' bodies are attached to their shells and cannot leave them.

HOW STRANGE!

The rings inside a snail's shell can be a good way to tell about how old it is. The shell that the snail is born with is in the middle of the spiral.

Snails are common in gardens! People often consider them pests because they eat vegetables like spinach and broccoli, which are loaded with the calcium they need for their growing shells.

UNDERWATER ANIMALS WITH ARMOR

Animals that live in the sea need to find ways to be safe from predators. That is why we find armored animals, such as crabs and lobsters, in the water. Oysters, clams, and other mollusks have shells too.

A crab is completely covered by a hard shell, even its legs. When it gets too big for its shell, it will molt. The crab will shed its old shell and grow a new one. A hermit crab is not a true crab. Its shell is softer than a regular crab's so it uses an empty shell to stay safe. As it grows, it will need to find bigger and bigger shells in which to live.

These brightly colored crabs are called Sally Lightfoot crabs. The young crabs start out darker, with red spots. As they molt, the red spots grow larger.

THE IMPORTANCE OF ARMOR

Animals have **adapted** in some amazing ways to keep themselves safe. Some animals are poisonous or have sharp teeth and claws. Others have colors or markings on their bodies to help them hide.

Armor is another way animals keep themselves safe. Armor makes it hard for predators to bite and eat an animal. It also keeps insects from biting and causing illness. Armor also can be useful if an animal lives in a place with lots of branches, thorns, or rocks that could hurt its body. Armor is important in so many ways to keep the animals on our planet alive and healthy!

GLOSSARY

adapt: To change to suit conditions.

bacteria: Tiny living things that can't be seen with the eye alone. Some bacteria cause illness or rotting, but others are helpful.

calcium: A soft, metallic element needed for growing bones and other animal parts.

defense: A feature of a living thing that helps keep it safe.

exoskeleton: The hard covering on the outside of an animal's body that holds and guards the soft insides.

gastropod: A kind of soft-bodied mollusk or shellfish that has a head and a single foot. The name means "belly footed."

habitat: The natural home for plants, animals, and other living things.

impenetrable: Impossible to get in or through.

mammal: Any warm-blooded animal whose babies drink milk and whose body is covered with hair or fur.

molt: To shed hair, feathers, shell, horns, or skin.

predator: Animals that kill other animals for food.

protect: To keep safe.

INDEX

A
AFRICA, 10, 12, 14
ALLIGATOR, 6, 10
ARMADILLO, 13, 14, 15
ASIA, 14

C
CICADA, 17
CLAM, 13, 20
CRAB, 5, 6, 20, 21
CROCODIE, 6, 10, 11

E
EXOSKELETON, 16, 17

G
GASTROPOD, 18

H
HIPPOPOTAMUS, 6, 7, 12

I
INSECTS, 16, 17

L
LION, 12
LIZARD, 10
LOBSTER, 6, 12, 20

M
MILLIPEDE, 13
MOLT, 17, 20, 21
MOLLUSK, 18, 20

P
PANGOLIN, 14, 15

S
SCALES, 4, 8, 10, 14, 15, 16
SCALLOP, 12
SHELL, 5, 8, 12, 18, 19, 20
SNAIL, 6, 13, 18, 19
SOUTH AMERICA, 15

T
TORTOISE, 8
TURTLE, 6, 8

WEBSITES

Due to the changing nature of Internet links, PowerKids Press has developed an online list of websites related to the subject of this book. This site is updated regularly. Please use this link to access the list: www.powerkidslinks.com/ccotak/armor